Original title:
The Comet Chronicles

Copyright © 2025 Creative Arts Management OÜ
All rights reserved.

Author: Sebastian Whitmore
ISBN HARDBACK: 978-1-80567-763-5
ISBN PAPERBACK: 978-1-80567-884-7

Luminescent Legacy

In the night sky, a bright parade,
Stars whisper jokes, fears fade.
Cosmic clowns with tails so grand,
Dancing dust, a cosmic band.

They trip on planets, swirl on moons,
Spinning tales like silly cartoons.
Gravity's missed its chance to play,
Laughing comets light the way.

Echoes Across the Void

In the vastness, echoes ring,
Galactic giggles, what joy they bring.
Nebulas swirl, a colorful tease,
Stars sharing secrets with cosmic ease.

Asteroids tumble, quite a show,
Whirling and twirling, watch them go!
A black hole's grumble, a funny phase,
Sucking in laughter for endless days.

A Celestial Serenade

Singing stars with a twinkling light,
Joke about darkness, it's quite the sight.
Winking meteors flash through air,
Throwing giggles, without a care.

A symphony of comets, a raucous cheer,
Dancing through space, no need for fear.
Laughter echoes through the astral scenes,
Galactic humor flows in cosmic streams.

Blazing Trails and Hidden Dreams

Chasing dreams on a fiery tail,
Trail mix of stars, a cosmic scale.
Planets spin in a playful race,
With each twist, comets lose their face.

Through the cosmos, they jump and leap,
Making friends with asteroids, not too deep.
Giggles abound in this starlit spree,
Where every cluster holds a funny spree.

Celestial Wanderer

Oh look, there's a wanderer, bright and bold,
Zipping through the cosmos, stories untold.
A tail made of stardust, glittering wide,
It sneezes and sparkles, what a wild ride!

With planets as playgrounds, it takes a dip,
Making friends with asteroids, what a trip!
They play tag and tumble, a cosmic ballet,
Laughing in loops, in their own milky way.

Starlit Whispers

In the night sky, whispers float and bounce,
Stars giggle and snicker, what a loud flounce!
They trade silly secrets, oh such a sight,
About comets and meteors clowning in flight.

One star tells a tale of a near-miss crash,
With a planet that slid by, just a flash!
They all burst with laughter, lightyears away,
As cosmic jokes brighten the galaxy's play.

A Dance Among the Stars

Come watch the dance, oh what a delight,
Stars twirl and spin in the velvet night.
The moons are the dancers, in gowns of light,
They waltz with the comets, oh, what a sight!

One twirl goes wrong, a starlet takes flight,
Smashing into a nebula, what a blight!
They laugh and recover, in a twinkling haze,
As space cheers them on with a million rays.

From Dust to Light

From dust to bright sparks, a journey anew,
With giggles and hiccups, as novas just do.
Brightening the dark with tales of their birth,
Spreading joy across the expanse of the Earth.

They chuckle at black holes, so grumpy and shy,
While spinning through galaxies, up high in the sky.
From nada to something, they light up the night,
Chasing their dreams, oh what a delight!

Luminous Secrets in the Dark

In the night sky, a wink of light,
A comet dances, what a sight!
It trips on stars, has no idea,
Yelling 'Oops!' to the Milky Way sphere.

Jetting off with a tail so bright,
It steals wishes, what a delight!
'Thank you!' says a falling star,
As it zooms past like a shooting car.

Only gathers dust from a cosmic sneeze,
Whirling and twirling with utmost ease.
Each stellar hop brings giggles and cheer,
While we wish for snacks and a little beer!

Eclipsed Dreams of the Cosmos

Under blankets of divine night,
While planets giggle from sheer delight.
A moon tries to blush, gets shy and cold,
As the sun tells stories, bright and bold.

Twinkling stars play hide and seek,
With a wink, they shine, oh so sleek.
Eclipsed dreams float in cosmic lanes,
While comets joke about passing lanes.

In cosmic cafes, they roast the sun,
With tales of worlds just for fun.
We sit back and chuckle, what a brew,
As time fluffers laugh at the cosmos anew!

Wandering Through Twinkling Memories

Cosmic travelers blink and sway,
On a tour through memories, hip-hip-hooray!
They reminisce about the time they fell,
In a black hole's joke, oh, what a swell!

With rings of laughter, they twirl in glee,
Past planets that giggle, dance, and spree.
'Got lost in space, did you hear?
A meteor told me, 'No worries, dear!'

Comets take selfies, strike a pose,
In a twinkling nebula, how it glows!
They send postcards from far-off lands,
While we laugh at stardust in our hands!

The Infinite Trail of Stardust

Space puppies chase a tail of light,
Making wishes in the cosmic night.
Dust to dust, they bark and play,
A trail of giggles in the Milky Way.

Asteroids chuckle, what a sight,
As they bounce past comets, shining bright.
'Thanks for the ride!' one comet will say,
'Just don't eat the stardust, it's here to stay!'

They drift on dreams, so sweet and bold,
Sharing secrets that never get old.
A sprinkle of laughter in the cosmic space,
Reminds us all to smile and embrace!

The Celestial Nomad

A traveler of the sky,
He zooms by without a sigh.
His tail a spark, his heart a glee,
Hitching rides on dreams of free.

He visits planets in a rush,
Leave behind a cosmic hush.
With aliens, he's quite the lad,
Sharing snacks, oh, isn't that rad?

Dodging rocks like a pro,
In a dance of cosmic flow.
Planets laugh and stars do giggle,
As he weaves through space with a wiggle.

Just when he thinks he's found his jam,
He trips over a space-time slam.
But with a wink and playful grin,
He's off to space, let the fun begin!

When Stars Align

When stars align, oh what a sight,
Dancing planets twirl in the night.
With little moons that spin and cheer,
They host a party, bring the beer!

Galaxies play bingo in style,
And comets race with a cheeky smile.
They swap their tails, a wild spree,
While asteroids sing in harmony.

Saturn's rings are hula hoops,
While Martians dig in cosmic soups.
The Milky Way joins in the fun,
A galactic bash for everyone!

But then a black hole yawns, oh dear,
Sucking in the snacks and beer.
Yet laughter echoes loud and clear,
In the vastness, joy still appears!

Threads of Cosmic Time

Thread by thread, the fabric flows,
Warping time in cosmic shows.
A stitch of laughter, a patch of light,
Creating dreams in the endless night.

The universes pull and tug,
Patching holes like a cosmic rug.
Time travelers strut in style,
With jokes that stretch for a thousand miles.

Knitting stars with threads of thought,
Twisting futures we never caught.
As we unravel, we find it clear,
Each loop's a giggle, raw and sincere.

So pull the yarn, let's weave away,
In the vastness where we all play.
Remember though, as you unwind,
A tangle can spark the best of finds!

Celestial Reflections

In the mirror of the night,
Stars giggle, dancing bright.
They reflect our quirks and plays,
Twinkling in their fancy ways.

The sun winks as it dips low,
While comets flash like a show.
With each glow, a dream ignites,
In cosmic puddles, giggles light.

Planets pose for selfies grand,
As they take turns, hand in hand.
With nebulae editing their smirk,
In space, it's laughter that does the work.

So gather 'round, the sky so wide,
Let's embrace the silly ride.
For in this dance of starry beams,
The universe chuckles at our dreams!

A Flicker That Crossed Time

In the night sky, a flash so bright,
It zoomed on by, what a silly sight!
A cosmic wink, from far away,
"Catch me if you can!" it seemed to say.

It danced with stars, did a little spin,
With a twinkling laugh, it wore a grin.
Time travelers gasped, as they took a peek,
"Next stop: 2025!" it gives a squeak.

Planetary pranks from a distant shore,
What happens next? It promises more.
Wormholes twist with giggles and glee,
As galaxies gather for a cosmic tea.

So here's to the flicker, so cheeky and bold,
A story worth sharing, a legend retold.
As it zips through the void, with laughter, unfurled,
We wave at the charm of the comical world!

Skyward Whirl

Up in the sky, there's a whirl and a twirl,
A mischievous spark gives the night a twirl.
With a whoosh and a giggle, it darts all around,
Leaving stardust giggles in a swirling mound.

Astronauts chuckle, pointing in delight,
"Is it a bird? A plane? Or just pure light?"
It tumbles and fumbles, such a jolly show,
Winking wildly, it steals the glow.

It loops through the clouds with a playful air,
Dancing with moonbeams, without a care.
Even the meteors roll on the floor,
As this whimsical flicker continues to soar.

In the vast universe, where humor runs free,
This starry spectacle is the life of the spree.
With laughter and light, it takes a grand flight,
In a skyward whirl that feels just right!

The Ascendant Spark

An ember on high, with a zany flair,
It glances and glimmers, with style so rare.
"Why so serious?" it seems to tease,
"Let's stir up the night, come on, let's please!"

It climbs and it dives, like a fish on land,
With wiggly wiggles, it's hard to withstand.
While planets giggle and comets applaud,
This shimmering prankster gives space a nod.

In a dizzying dash, it sparks and it shakes,
A splash of starlight that utterly wakes.
Extraterrestrials join in the fun,
Racing with laughter, no need to outrun.

So up we look, with wonder and cheer,
At the ascendant spark, we hold so dear.
It's a cosmic ballet with jokes in the air,
A wacky adventure beyond compare!

Celestial Farewells

As meteors shower, we gather around,
Parting is sweet, let laughter abound.
With a nod and a wink, our friends take the flight,
Grinning and chuckling, into the night.

"Goodbye for now!" shouts a blast of light,
"I'll send postcards; don't shed a tear tonight!"
Orbiting home, their spirits will soar,
With tales of tomfoolery, forever in store.

In the cosmic embrace, as distances grow,
Stars kiss the moon; a tender hello.
They've promised to return, be it soon or late,
With stories of giggles; we simply can't wait.

So here's to the journeys beyond our own skies,
With each celestial farewell whispered in sighs.
As laughter rings out in the great cosmic shell,
We treasure the moments and bid them farewell!

Beneath the Astral Canopy

Beneath the stars, a giant quirk,
Aliens dance with quite a smirk.
A spaceship broke, it spun around,
While astronauts just fell down!

Galactic games of hide and seek,
Space squirrels dart, they squeak and peek.
A cosmic cat, with whiskers wide,
Chased all the meteors that glide.

Planets wobble in a groove,
Saturn's rings just can't lose their move.
Asteroids gather for a snack,
Oh, what a spacey Zodiac!

A comet zooms, it slips and slides,
Unruly through the cosmic tides.
Waving to stars, it trips the light,
"Oops!" it yells, "Let's dance all night!"

Light's Eclipsed Journey

A star was late, missed its own show,
"Sorry, folks, I had to go slow!"
It tripped on a cloud, fell in a beam,
And ended up in a moonlit dream.

Planets giggled at the blunder,
"Did you hear that?" they whispered under.
While light-years passed, they played a prank,
Made the sun glow pink, oh how they sank!

A comet tried to photobomb,
With a goofy face, like a cartoon charm.
But the Milky Way just rolled its eyes,
"Here we go again—so many surprise!"

Spaceships raced, helmets askew,
Zooming through asteroids, out of the blue.
The pilot sighed, "Can we take a break?
I'm steering this thing like it's a cake!"

Starborn Stories

Once in space, a tale was spun,
Of a star who thought it could run!
It jogged so hard, it lost its glow,
Now it twinkles very slow.

Meteor showers had a blast,
As wishes flew—these moments last.
One wished for cookies, one wished for cake,
Now they're feasting, for goodness' sake!

Aliens wrote a spacey book,
Filled with secrets, just take a look.
Chapter one: how to dance in space,
But netted arms? Not quite in place!

A celestial bard strummed a song,
His notes flew high, oh so long.
But even with stars, he missed a beat,
Now they all dance—two left feet!

Descent of the Celestial Traveler

A ship descended, soft and slow,
With crew all dressed in bright, bold glow.
They thought they'd land on Mars, it's true,
Instead, they crashed in a zoo—oh boo!

"Spacesuits do not fit with pandas,"
One cried, "And zebras give us handed plans!"
A giraffe giggled, high and proud,
"Welcome to Earth, join the crowd!"

They tried to build a rocket there,
But llamas chewed on parts with flair.
"Use hay instead!" they all decreed,
Now it travels at llama speed!

The traveler laughed, what a delight,
To lose his path and find this sight.
In space, they'd missed the silly play,
But here on Earth, they'd laugh all day!

Odes to the Unseen Traveler

A traveler zooms by, kicking up dust,
With wobbly wheels, it's a starry must.
It shimmies and shakes, makes funny sounds,
While alien cats chase it all around.

Spinning like pizza, it twirls through space,
In comical leaps, it's quite the race.
A wink from a planet, a nudge from the moon,
Together they giggle, with interstellar tune.

Rockets go whizzing, they lose track and spin,
They trip over comet tails, oh where to begin?
With hiccups and chuckles, the cosmos unite,
Painting the universe with laughter so bright.

On this odd journey, with stars for a map,
Each detour a joke, each black hole a trap.
Through giggles and glares, the voyage unfolds,
With tales of the unseen, forever retold.

Nebula's Embrace

In a swirl of colors, the gas clouds collide,
A party of photons, where secrets reside.
They dance and they giggle, in a cosmic ballet,
Tickling the dark like a cheeky hooray.

Stars pop like popcorn, a burst of delight,
They twinkle and tumble, oh what a sight!
With nebulous snickers, they cover their eyes,
As asteroids juggle, much to their surprise.

The universe whispers, "Join in the fun!"
Planets play hopscotch, all under the sun.
With rings made of chocolate, oh what a dream,
Nebulas laughing like a well-rehearsed team.

So embrace the confusion, the chaos, the mirth,
From swirling creations to comical birth.
In this wacky expanse, joy's never a waste,
For each twinkling shadow wears laughter's embrace.

Shadows of the Last Star

In the corner of space, where shadows creep,
Lurks the last shining star, ready to leap.
It sneezes, it twinkles, and giggles so bright,
While planets roll by, drawn to the light.

The shadows all whisper, "What's going on?"
As comets play tag from dusk until dawn.
They've donned silly hats, each one with a grin,
Daring the twilight to let the fun in.

Asteroids tumble, trying to dance,
In a madcap routine, they take every chance.
With a flop and a spin, they create quite the show,
While the last star chuckles, "Give it a go!"

So under this last glow, where shadows entwine,
Laughter echoes across galaxies, sweet, so divine.
For in space's embrace, we all share a laugh,
In the cosmic theater, we find our own path.

Cosmic Histories Untold

Once upon a time, in galaxies far,
Dreams were discovered by a runaway car.
Zooming through stardust, with a honk and a beep,
It gathered up laughter, in a cosmic sweep.

With stories of aliens, as silly as pie,
They giggled at comets, watched them whoosh by.
In the annals of space, they scribbled with glee,
Recording the mischief of the galaxy's spree.

Planets threw parties with jellybean cores,
While funny-faced moons rattled their roars.
With laughter as fuel, they traveled through night,
Turning dark voids into pure delight.

In the records of space, where histories mix,
Are tales spun from stardust that everyone picks.
For cosmic chronicles, both bright and bold,
Are filled with this laughter, eternally told.

Dance of Light and Shadow

In the sky, a bright show,
Twinkling lights put on a glow.
Dancing through the midnight air,
Laughter floats without a care.

Whirling bits of cosmic cheer,
Whispers echo, loud and clear.
Shooting stars with silly names,
Playing oh-so-funny games.

Little giggles in the dark,
Each one shines, a playful spark.
They spin like kids in a race,
Winking down with a silly face.

So when you gaze at night's dome,
Know those lights are not alone.
They laugh and dance above our heads,
Chasing dreams, where fun still spreads.

Starlit Echoes

In a night where wishes fly,
Silly giggles dance up high.
Stars are whispering their lines,
Echoing with cheeky signs.

Each twinkle's got a snappy joke,
Cracking up as stardust spoke.
They play hide-and-seek, it's true,
"Catch me if you can!" they boo.

Galactic games on cosmic slides,
Where mischief sparkles and abides.
Planets play the flute and drum,
Making tunes that go 'Bum Bum!'

So look up with a laughing heart,
Let the joy of night impart.
For in the silvers and the blues,
Are jokes and giggles just for you.

A Comet's Soliloquy

A flash of light, oh what a sight,
Made a vow to dance tonight.
Swirling through the velvet sea,
"Look at me, I'm wild and free!"

With a tail that sways and glows,
It jests and jives, oh how it flows.
"Don't blink twice or I'll be missed,
Shooting past, like foggy mist!"

It chats with moons, and stars it teases,
In cosmic talks, it laughs and pleases.
"Did you hear what Venus said?
I swear she flipped, just like a thread!"

This comet spins through endless skies,
With bubbly tales and winking eyes.
So when you see that fleeting trail,
Know it's just comedy on a cosmic scale.

Remnants of Celestial Visits

An asteroid strolled past my yard,
With a chuckle, it wasn't hard.
"Excuse me, mate, I'm just a guest,
Dropping by to show my zest!"

Dusty trails and little crumbs,
It giggled softly, "Aren't I fun?"
A nudge from Mars called out in glee,
"Join us here, it's quite a spree!"

Crumbs of starlight here and there,
Twinkling giggles fill the air.
"Hope you saved a wish for me,
I love the jokes from galaxy!"

So when the night seems gloom and dull,
Just remember the cosmic pull.
For all those pieces flung away,
Come back to smile and dance and play.

Songs of the Midnight Sky

Inky blobs with tails so bright,
Chasing dreams with all their might,
They giggle as they zoom around,
A cosmic dance without a sound.

Wobbling stars, a clumsy bunch,
They munch on space-food for their lunch,
Silly sounds they make while eating,
Like popcorn popping, quite defeating.

Galaxies twirl in dizzy spins,
Racing rocks with goofy grins,
Each one claims they're the fastest here,
But trips and falls bring raucous cheer.

With a flick and a flashy twist,
They gather 'round for a cosmic tryst,
A jovial group that can't seem to hide,
Laughing as they streak in astral pride.

Celestial Whirl

Bouncing balls of light so free,
In a twisty, whirly spree,
They race through space, left and right,
Playing tag in the deep, dark night.

Asteroids in jammies twirl,
They stumble and laugh, oh what a whirl!
Meteor showers rain on down,
The silliest game in the starry town.

Comets sing, a tuneful blur,
Sctatching heads, "What's that fur?"
Turned out it's just their fluffy tails,
Flapping furiously as joy prevails!

Planets wobble, claiming fame,
In this cosmic, playful game,
Who knew that space could be so fun?
Where laughter shines brighter than the sun.

Phantoms of the Starlit Sea

Shadows dance on waves of light,
Ghostly laughter, a joyful sight,
They surf on beams, with quickened zest,
Calling friends, inviting the best.

Galaxy fish with glittering scales,
Tell stories of cosmic gales,
Splashes of laughter echo so loud,
Chasing tails through the ghostly crowd.

Whimsical whales in shimmering hues,
Bop along to their silly tunes,
With every flip, their joy ignites,
A stellar party in mystical nights.

So come and join this giddy spree,
Phantoms frolic, wild and free,
In this magical, starry expanse,
Where laughter reigns and all will dance.

Driftwood on Cosmic Shores

Lumbering logs with glittering vibes,
Floating stories from the starry tribes,
They drift along with whimsical flair,
    Telling tales of cosmic air.

With splashes of mirth, they recount the times,
    When meteors fell like silly chimes,
    Each one giggles at silly errors,
    Dancing past orbital terrors.

Down the river of twinkling lights,
They sing ballads to shimmering heights,
Bouncing on waves made of pastel dreams,
    Life is sweet, bursting at the seams!

Cosmic shores of laughter and glee,
Where driftwood logs wade poolside tea,
All are welcome in this merry realm,
As humor guides this timeless helm.

Flickering Tales of the Cosmos

In a galaxy wide with a wink and a grin,
Dancing stars invite mischief, let the fun begin.
Planets are twirling in a cosmic ballet,
While asteroids are rapping in a comical way.

Aliens slip on banana peels with style,
Searching for laughter across the light mile.
They juggle comets like they're easy as pie,
Making each journey a giggle and sigh.

Moonbeams tickle space bunnies, fluffy and bright,
Playing tag with stardust, oh what a sight!
Galactic giggles echo through vast skies,
As nebulae chuckle in colorful ties.

From black holes that burp to supernovas that sneeze,
Space is a party, bringing all to their knees.
Laughter in starlight, oh what a grand chase,
Join these funny tales from the cosmic space!

A Voyage in Starlight

Once on a ship made of candy and dreams,
Sailing through glittery starlight beams.
Captain Gigglepants at the helm so bold,
With a parrot named Snickers, both silly and old.

Through cosmic swirls and jellybean dew,
They chased shooting stars, a magical crew.
Every bump in the void, a chuckle, a cheer,
As space whales sang songs for all to hear.

Navigating plums and cotton candy clouds,
This wacky adventure drew in big crowds.
They played hopscotch on planets round,
Leaving trails of laughter wherever they found.

With a wink from the sun and a twirl of a moon,
They danced through the cosmos, a whimsical tune.
Back to their world with stories to share,
Of starlight voyages from here to nowhere!

Radiant Trails of Wonder

In the depths of the night where rockets zoom high,
A band of comets throws a glowing pie.
They giggle and zoom with laughter in tow,
Leaving trails of delight wherever they go.

They race with satellites, play bumper in space,
Making friends with a moon, oh what a warm place!
A cosmic parade of fun and allure,
Each light a reminder, adventure is sure.

Space mice in spacesuits, dancing with glee,
Finding cheese in the heavens, oh how carefree!
Galaxies spin as if caught in a tale,
While stars wink and nudge as they soar without fail.

At twilight the giggles of starlings unite,
Creating a symphony of joy, pure delight.
In a universe painted with laughter and light,
They spread radiant trails of wonder, so bright!

Whispers from the Asteroid Belt

Deep in the belt, where rocks like to play,
Asteroids chatter in their bumpy ballet.
"Hey, watch this!" one shouts, with a leap and a spin,
While others just giggle as they tumble in.

Each rock has a story, each jolt a surprise,
Twinkling at passing ships with mischievous eyes.
They prank passing comets, with jokes made of stone,
Creating a ruckus in their orbit of bone.

From the smallest pebble to the grandest of boulders,
All share their laughter as the universe smolders.
They have snack time with dark matter cups,
Bantering away as they eat cosmic pups.

In a space filled with whispers, a joyous parade,
Asteroids frolic in the twilight cascade.
With chuckles and whispers from each rocky friend,
The humor of the cosmos will never quite end!

Dreams in Astral Dust

In a night full of dreams, we make a plan,
To hitch a ride on a space-faring van.
We'll sprinkle some stardust, make our mark,
And bounce past the moon like a sparkly lark.

With giggles we zoom through the Milky Way,
Poking the stars, in a cosmic ballet.
A twisty tail spins, like a comet's dance,
We might even find aliens while in a trance.

They sip on starlight, with laughter and cheer,
Offering us moon pies, oh isn't that clear?
But we're too busy enjoying the ride,
As laughter and echoes of joy collide.

So hold onto your hats, let's soar and spin,
Every twist and turn brings a huge goofy grin.
In dreams of astral dust, we'll forever stay,
Where fun meets the cosmos in a silly ballet.

The Stellar Messenger

A quirky star decided to text and beam,
Whispering secrets of a cosmic dream.
"Hey, Earthlings! Want to join my parade?
I'll show you the wonders that the heavens made!"

With a wink and a twinkle, it beckoned with flair,
Inviting us all to a dance in midair.
We twirled with the planets, forgot about lunch,
Bounced off shooting stars, what a funky bunch!

Messages giggled and planets did spin,
As we high-fived the asteroids, letting joy in.
"Let's launch some wishes on this glorious ride,
In this stellar spree, we'll laugh and abide!"

So if you hear laughter in the cosmic tide,
Know it's the star sending fun with pride.
We're rollercoaster riders in the void's gleam,
On a quest for giggles, living our dream.

Fading Echoes of a Distant Star

Once a star flickered, oh what a sight,
Winking through space, left and right.
It cracked a joke, but we missed the punch,
So we howled with laughter, a cosmic brunch!

Echoes came tumbling, a giggly decree,
Transmitting the silliness, just between you and me.
"If you can hear this, do a funky dance,
And let the universe give your dreams a chance!"

With starry confetti swirling about,
We created our own noisy clout.
The echoes bounced back like a cosmic choir,
Tickling our ribs, sparking joy's fire!

So when a distant light begins to fade,
Remember the laughter, the tricks it played.
For every giggle fades into the night,
While echoes remember our silly delight.

Chronicles of Light and Shadow

In a realm of shadows where sunlight plays,
Danced a silly creature in moonbeam rays.
It juggled meteors and shared a bright grin,
Inviting the world to join in the spin.

"Why fear the dark when you can boogie here?
Just grab a space snack, let go of that fear!"
With a playful bounce, it stole the scene,
Making the void feel more like a dream.

So come twirl with the shadows, let laughter reign,
Grab a comet-net, let's catch the strange chain.
Flip through constellations, make a silly wish,
And share those goofy laughs, that's the cosmic dish!

From light into shadow, a giggle parade,
Chronicles woven with memories made.
So dance through the cosmos, let joy unfurl,
In the light and the shadow, let laughter swirl!

The Pulse of the Universe

In space, there's a dancing star,
It wobbles and jiggles from afar.
It spins with a grin and twirls around,
Making funny faces, oh what a sound!

Globular galaxies share their jokes,
While black holes laugh, surrounded by blokes.
The neutron stars clap, the planets all cheer,
As light-years of laughter just fill the sphere.

Asteroids wear hats, they strut and parade,
While comets throw sparkles like petticoat shade.
In this cosmic ball, joy bursts like a bubble,
And even the vacuum feels light and not trouble.

So join in the fun, and take a good peek,
At this wild universe, where joy's never meek.
With humor so bright, it lights up the void,
In the pulse of existence, we all feel overjoyed!

Comet's Lament

There once was a comet, quite long and quite wide,
Who lost all its flair on a cosmic ride.
It tripped on the orbits, missed planets galore,
Now it grumbles in space, feeling quite poor.

"Oh heavens!" it sighs, "I wanted to glow,
Now I'm just dust, with nowhere to go."
Star friends all chuckle, the meteors tease,
"Just brush off that stardust, do as you please!"

But our comet kept crying, oh woe is my fate,
Stuck in the gloom, it peered down with hate.
"Let's throw a big party!" said Mercury bright,
And suddenly, laughter lit up the night.

With confetti of starlight and laughter so bold,
The comet was cheered, and felt bright as gold.
Now it zips through the skies, with a smile in tow,
A comet that learned how to dance in the glow!

The Cosmic Canvas

In the artful expanse where the galaxies meet,
Stars splash their colors, oh what a treat!
Nebulae swirl, painting skies with delight,
While cosmic brush strokes create wonder at night.

Each planet a dot, in the painter's grand scheme,
With moons that all giggle in luminous gleam.
Black holes spill secrets, and starfields applaud,
As comets zip past, feeling quite awed.

"Let's splash on some laughter!" the asteroids shout,
"Let's paint silly faces and swirl all about!"
So they flicked their dust and they twirled in the air,
Creating a masterpiece, beyond all compare.

With giggles and sparkles, the canvas unfurled,
A canvas of humor, enchanting the world.
In cosmic creation, joy splatters and glares,
In this funny universe, laughter is rare!

Journey Through the Starlit Veil

Embarking on voyages through silvery skies,
With stardust for snacks and a wink in their eyes.
Astronauts giggle as they float through the air,
In their silly space suits, they dance without care.

Planets wink back with mischievous glee,
While moons tell stories from ages we see.
"Don't trip on the comets!" a voice calls with cheer,
"Or you'll tumble through space with a quizzical sneer."

Galaxies swirl, like a dizzying ride,
As meteors whistle, and supernova glide.
The starship now wobbles, it careens like a kite,
As laughter erupts in the vastness of night.

Through the starlit veil, adventures unfold,
With each silly moment, new tales to be told.
In this cosmic funhouse, where mirth is our sail,
We relish the wonders of our light-hearted trail!

The Astral Archipelago

In the sky, a pizza slice,
Floating by, what a nice surprise!
Stars said, 'We're just here for snacks!'
Planetary chefs in cosmic hats.

Asteroids like bowling balls,
Rolling past with loud, weird calls.
Black holes open for a brief dance,
Wormholes working on their prance.

Galaxies twirl like swirling swirls,
Space dust sprinkled with sparkly pearls.
Aliens giggle, pull weird faces,
As they zoom through starry spaces.

So if you catch a shooting star,
Just wave and shout, "Hey there, bizarre!"
The universe laughs, it's quite the show,
In this archipelago, cosmic and slow.

Threads of Infinity

In a loom of cosmic thread,
Space knitters craft with joy and dread.
Stitching stars with fuzzy yarn,
Mistakes are fun, they say, 'No harm!'

Quasars twinkle in rows so bright,
Knit one, purl two, it feels just right.
Satellites dodge a dropping stitch,
Galactic patterns are quite the glitch.

With every thread, the tales unwind,
Of asteroids lost and suns that shined.
Black holes pull, but we won't relent,
Knit on, dear friend, with comet scent.

So when you see that twinkling bright,
Think of the stitches weaving the night.
In this cosmic shop, where yarns collide,
Threads of infinity, woven with pride.

Light's Journey Through Darkness

Light took a bus through shades of night,
With characters that gave quite a fright.
Shadow critics counting each beam,
'This glow's too flashy,' they scream.

They played cards with photons, so quick,
Made bets on who'd take the next flick.
A glowstick threw a party nearby,
While darkness sighed, 'Oh my, oh my!'

As light laughed, it bounced on the wall,
Flickering 'round the shadowed hall.
Chasing giggles and silly songs,
It danced through the void, where it belongs.

So if you see a ray trying to seize,
The dark for a laugh, with such ease,
Just know it's light, in joy it boasts,
A playful journey that loves to toast.

Cosmic Footprints on the Soil of Time

In the sand of time, there's a print so bold,
Made by aliens, or so I'm told.
They danced on planets, wiggled their toes,
Leaving laughter wherever they go.

Stars look down at the cosmic scene,
'What's that?' they blink, 'Oh! Look at it gleam!'
Footprints lead to a pizza place,
With toppings from every faraway space.

The time travelers trip over cosmic rocks,
Wearing mismatched shoes like ancient flocks.
In starlit puddles, playful reflections,
Cosmic humor in all its directions.

So if you wander through time's soft sand,
And see those prints that were etched by hand,
Just follow the giggles in the starlit night,
To a pizza party, full of delight!

A Flicker in the Cosmic Sea

A spark danced brightly, so spry and free,
It tickled the stars, oh wittily!
Asteroids giggled as they swirled around,
Whispering secrets in a playful sound.

Planets had parties, all dressed in style,
With comets in tuxedos, they danced a while.
Saturn spun tunes with its rings in tow,
While Jupiter laughed, stealing the show!

Each shooting star in a zany race,
Chasing their tails in a playful chase.
The moon just grinned, with a chuckle so bright,
As the cosmos grooved on that magical night.

In this lively ballroom of dust and glee,
Celestial bodies wobbled with glee.
A flicker of chaos, a spark of delight,
In the grand dance of stars under cosmic light.

Dreams Carved in Light

In the sky's canvas, dreams took flight,
Carved in stardust, shimmering bright.
Funny whispers echoed from afar,
As cosmic critters danced 'neath a star.

A galaxy chef whipped comets to fry,
While aliens chuckled, oh my, oh my!
Nebulas tossed rainbow confetti high,
While shooting stars giggled with a twinkle in the eye.

Meteorites skated on light beams so slick,
Making wishes and dreams with the flick of a trick.
The sun pulled a prank, turned day into night,
Sending shadows away in a flash of sheer light.

These whimsical wonders, oh, what a sight!
In the vast velvet sky, a fanciful flight.
Where laughter lingers, and giggles take flight,
Dreams are spun in the fabric of light.

Celestial Harbinger's Farewell

With a wink and a wave, the harbinger sighed,
As planets and stars all giggled and pried.
"Twirling in chaos, who knew this could be?
Dancing with meteors, oh, what a spree!"

In the twilight's glow, they held a parade,
With bouncing comets making memories laid.
Asteroids juggled, with a grin so wide,
As the cosmos burst forth, full of pride.

"Farewell, my friends, it's time to disperse,
Let's spin tales of laughter, and not a curse!"
So they sang and they twirled in the cosmic breeze,
Painting the sky with chuckles and ease.

With a final twinkle, the harbinger soared,
Leaving behind joy that the stars ever adored.
A laugh in the silence, an echo to last,
In the memory of light, where the good times blast.

Paths of Light and Shadow

Down the paths where shadows play,
And light bursts forth in a zany ballet.
Planets peeked out from their cozy nests,
Playing tag with beams, they laughed with zest.

Lunar bunnies hopped on beams of gold,
While solar squirrels made mischief bold.
Shooting stars raced, with trails so bright,
As giggles echoed through the velvet night.

Galaxies swirled in a swirling spree,
Dancing through darkness, wild and free.
They sketched silly stories in the dark,
With sparks of laughter igniting a spark.

In this cosmic playground, a joyous cheer,
Where light and shadow danced without fear.
In paths unknown, a whimsical blend,
Of giggles and grins that never end.

The Wandering Light

A flash zooms past, oh what a sight,
With all its flair, it takes to flight.
Waving to planets, making them grin,
In cosmic chaos, it twirls like a pinwheel.

It swirls through stars, a playful tease,
Tickling the moons, with the greatest of ease.
With a wink and a blink, it's gone in a flash,
Leaving behind a trail, a glittery splash.

Where's it off to? Can't quite tell,
Maybe to party with the great Martian swell.
Laughing with asteroids, a comedic charade,
In this vast universe, such fun is portrayed.

So watch the sky, for that silly light,
With dreams and giggles, it dances at night.
In the grand cosmic circus, it shines so bright,
A jester of wonders, a pure delight.

Celestial Odyssey

A spaceship slips, with goofy grace,
Zooming past in interstellar space.
Its captain laughs, spills juice on his socks,
As meteors knock, "What are you, rocks?"

Pluto rolls by, wearing a hat,
Says, "I'm a planet! Can you handle that?"
The Milky Way giggles, an old cosmic friend,
As the ship spins 'round, it's a laugh to the end.

Stars take a bow, in a twinkling queue,
Shooting star wishes? Oh, what a few!
With every flip, there's a dance-off to claim,
Who can fly straight? It's all just a game.

So join this ride, let's laugh and shout,
In this whacky parade, we never pout.
The universe whispers, with each little twirl,
In this silly grandeur, oh what a whirl!

Secrets of the Night Sky

Under the cloak of evening's dark shade,
Starlight giggles, secrets displayed.
Constellations whisper, trading their charms,
While comets zoom in, raising alarms.

"Oh dear!" says Orion, "Where's my left arm?"
With a chuckle, he waves, "Oh, it causes no harm!"
Sirius snickers, wagging its tail,
While the moon pulls faces, without any fail.

Galaxies twirl in this night-time ball,
Spinning together, never to fall.
A winking Venus plays hide-and-seek,
"Catch me, if you can!" it playfully squeaks.

So, grab some popcorn and gaze up high,
For laughter and joy beneath the sky.
In this cosmic dance, so wild and bright,
The secrets unfold in the soft, moonlit night.

Celestial Vagabond

A rogue star wanders, straying afar,
With hefty dreams of becoming a star.
It bumps into planets, spinning so free,
"Whoa, slow down! Save some for me!"

With cosmic ballets, it twirls and leaps,
Through asteroid fields, where the universe sleeps.
Zipping past comets, it cracks up in mirth,
An intergalactic jester, for all it's worth.

"Where's my next stop? A black hole, perhaps?"
It chuckles and giggles, like silly mishaps.
The dust and the gas make a carnival scene,
As stars look on, "Oh, what could it mean?"

So join the parade, in your fanciest vibes,
For this galactic romp, it surely describes,
The life of a wanderer, free and unbound,
In this playground of light, joy's always around.

Voyage of the Shining Harbinger

In sky's grand theater, they took flight,
Polka-dotted ships with sails so bright.
They danced around stars like disco balls,
Chasing a comet, oh, what a haul!

They spilled space juice, oh what a sight,
As aliens chuckled in sheer delight.
With sandwiches floating, a cosmic feast,
'Where's the punchline?' said the curious beast.

Asteroids tossed like confetti rain,
Spaceship laughter, no room for pain.
A Captain named Quirky spun like a top,
While his crew did the moonwalk, non-stop!

Through wormholes wild, they zipped and zoomed,
In a ballet of nonsense, humor bloomed.
With every giggle, they gained some speed,
These cosmic clowns were born to lead!

The Ghost of Stellar Paths

On a midnight ride with a ghostly vibe,
An ectoplasmic friend joined the jive.
Floating through stars with a grin so wide,
He told silly tales of the galactic tide.

He claimed to know Martians who loved to dance,
And Jupiter's rings, the best in France.
With cosmic hiccups, he laughed and swayed,
'Can you believe I used to be afraid?'

Stars winked at us in the space-age night,
Navigating paths that glimmered bright.
'It's all a joke,' the ghost said with glee,
'Just ask the asteroids, they agree!'

So we sailed past planets, laughed with glee,
While distant galaxies all joined the spree.
In the humorous void, we found our grace,
What a silly, starry embrace!

Constellations of Fate

In the tapestry of stars, funny shapes abound,
Like a cat in a hat, and a dog twirling round.
They plotted their paths with cosmic flair,
While sagas of laughter filled the air.

Orion fought off the tickling winds,
While Canis Major played cards with his friends.
A starry debate on who flew the best,
Gave birth to a supernova jest.

Zodiac signs dropped their regal pose,
For a cosmic dance-off nobody knows.
With glittering tails, they twirled and spun,
In a stellar ballet, oh, what fun!

As the universe giggled, we joined the craze,
Mapping the stars in hilarious ways.
Constellations, oh, what stories they weave,
In the space of mirth, we all believe!

Celestial Secrets Unraveled

Deep in the cosmos, where secrets reside,
A group of stars took a daring ride.
With whispers of laughter and winks of light,
They set out to conquer the endless night.

'What do you call a black hole's joke?'
Asked a cheeky nova with a playful poke.
'Absurdly funny, but it can't explain,
How it swallows everything, not a grain!'

They gathered round meteors, swirling with glee,
As comets played tag, wild and free.
'Tell us the secret to laughter's embrace,'
Said a bold quasar, ready for space.

And through cosmic riddles, they found their way,
As galactic giggles turned night into day.
In the heart of the stars, where joy is true,
They unveiled the secrets that sparkles imbue!

The Sky's Forgotten Traveler

Once there was a traveler, light as a breeze,
He flew past the planets with the greatest of ease.
He wanted to meet aliens, oh what a sight,
But they mistook him for a shooting star at night.

He waved at the asteroids, bumped into one,
"Oops, my bad!" he laughed, thinking it was fun.
But space is a vacuum, it echoed his jokes,
And the stars just twinkled, ignoring the bloke.

With snacks made of stardust and drinks from a ring,
He danced with the meteors, they formed a swing.
But one misstep, and into a black hole,
He dove with a giggle, losing all control.

Where did he end up? No one really knows,
But cosmic jokes are where anything goes!
He's still out there laughing, bright as a sun,
The universe chuckles at the traveler's fun.

A Journey Beyond the Moon

A rocket sat ready with its lunchbox packed,
To journey beyond, it was quite the act.
With ice cream and comets, oh what a treat,
Its engine revved up for a fun cosmic feat.

Past the moon's cheesy grin, they soared on high,
Playing tag with craters, both daring and spry.
"Oh look!" shouted Rocket, "It's a flying cow!"
But it turned out to be space debris — wow.

With each star they passed, it tickled their fancies,
They giggled through meteors, executing prances.
A solar flare popped like a party balloon,
And Rocket just giggled, "We'll be home soon!"

Though they missed home-cooked meals and the sun's warm glow,
They found laughter in space made their hearts overflow.
As they soared through the galaxy, bright and bold,
They wrote funny tales, celestial and gold.

Celestia's Last Song

One night in the cosmos, a star felt quite bold,
She started to sing, her voice bright and gold.
But the planets all laughed, took it lightheartedly,
As she tripped on her notes, grinning heartily.

"Stop that racket!" huffed Saturn, quite out of tune,
But couldn't resist and began to loop-de-loop soon.
The moons all joined in, with a rhythm so merry,
They twirled and they spun, like a cosmic fairy.

Comets cut in with their swishy bright tails,
Dancing and laughing, ignoring their trails.
"Let's start a band!" squeaked a brave little star,
They jammed through the cosmos, no matter how far.

But alas, all good things must end in a freeze,
As Celestia's notes tumbled down like the leaves.
Now starlight is silent, but the laughter remains,
A song lost in space, in the heart it retains.

Fragments of a Celestial Tale

In the heart of the void, a fragment once fell,
It shouted, "I'm a comet! Oh do wish me well!"
But it turned out to be a confused piece of junk,
Declaring itself royalty, all shiny and funk.

"Let's build a spaceship made of candy and dreams!"
It rallied up stardust, amidst cosmic beams.
Along came a spaceship made of old shoes,
With aliens who danced, ignoring the blues.

They traveled through orbits, quite colorful scenes,
With laughter and giggles, they filled the machines.
But when they hit Pluto, the junk claimed the throne,
Declaring itself king, all laughs and all groans.

Now legend declares of that hilarious flight,
Of a comet-like junk, dancing through the night.
And if you look closely, in the dark's gentle veil,
You might just hear whispers of fragments' fine tale.

Celestial Revelations

A space cat floated by, oh what a sight,
With a cape made of stars, it danced in delight.
It chased after meteors, with tails all aglow,
Saying, "Catch me if you can, but you already know!"

Planets were laughing, with rings they would swing,
While asteroids juggled, their cosmic bling.
In this stellar circus, the universe spun,
Where laughter and light made chaos seem fun.

Rockets in tutus performed on a dime,
Doing pirouettes in the fabric of time.
At such a vast scale, joy bubbled and grew,
Space parties were hosted by creatures askew.

Galactic confetti rained down from above,
As aliens toasted with drinks full of love.
"Oh, look at that star! What a terrible hit!"
Laughter was cosmic, not one soul could quit!

Cosmic Dances in Silence

A planet spun round, in a purple tutu,
While asteroids giggled, calling out, "Woohoo!"
Stars lined up neatly, in a conga parade,
Winking at comets that steadily swayed.

Nebulas twirled, in sparkly delight,
While black holes covered their eyes in fright.
"Don't get too close!" shouted a star in green,
"We aim to amuse, not to cause a scene!"

With space pies flying, and space cakes so sweet,
Zombies danced cha-cha, with hurtling debris fleet.
Gravity shrugged, as it joined in the fun,
Making sure every wink weighed a ton!

Across the vast void, laughter rang clear,
Echoing softly for all to hear.
Who knew the cosmos could tickle the soul?
Exploding with giggles, a celestial roll!

Fragments of a Star's Dream

In a dream of starlight, a quasar appeared,
Wearing mismatched socks, how wonderfully weird!
It swung on a meteor, whistling a tune,
While gas clouds nodded, under the moon.

A shooting star hiccupped, then burped with a grin,
"Excuse me, dear planets, where do I begin?"
With stardust in coffee and wit on the side,
A galaxy chuckled, enjoying the ride.

Blurry-eyed comets collided, what fun!
"Let's ramble around until we ensure we run!"
The universe snickered, lighting up the sky,
In shards of bright laughter, they aimed to fly high.

As memories shimmered, like jewels in the dark,
The cosmos reminded us, all holds a spark.
Within this vast dream of peculiar delight,
Stars found their brightness, igniting the night!

Under the Comet's Gaze

Under the gaze of a comet quite sly,
A duo of aliens prepared to fly high.
With mismatched antennas, they jumped around,
Claiming the moon was the silliest ground.

"Look at those craters, like cheese from a feast!
We'll serve them at parties; oh, what a beast!"
With giggles and wiggles, they bounced on the scene,
Making music from stars, a cosmic machine.

"Be careful!" said Jupiter, "or you might just fall,
But that might be useful; we'll all have a ball!"
With every grand misstep, the laughter would soar,
As comets lit trails, they yearned for much more.

So under the comet, they danced through the night,
Spreading their silliness, oh what a sight!
With infinite joy, they whirled and they spun,
In a universe where humor's never outdone!

The Alchemist of Stardust

In a lab of moonlit beams,
Potions bubble, dreamlike themes.
Mixing laughter with a star,
Silly mishaps, bizarre and far.

A sprinkle here, a dash of glee,
Turning night into a spree.
With every twist, a giggle grows,
Watch out for those glowing toes!

Jars of wishes on the shelf,
"Be careful, don't trip, you might warp yourself!"
The alchemist dances, spinning light,
Creating chaos 'til dawn's first sight.

So if you see a comet's tail,
It's just his hair, blown by the gale.
For in the cosmos, what a sight,
Alchemy of fun, pure delight!

Celestial Melodies at Dawn

When stars decide to hum a tune,
They wake the sun to dance by noon.
A jolly jig across the sky,
As planets giggle, spinning high.

With cosmic horns and comets bright,
They play all night, oh what a sight!
Shooting stars join in the fun,
While moons croon softly, one by one.

Imagine stardust serenades,
While asteroids throw grand parades.
The dawn breaks with a whimsical cheer,
Echoing laughter, far and near.

As lunars strum their new guitar,
They dream of being a pop star!
In the morning, they'll fade away,
But their cosmic concert makes my day!

Chronicles of the Wandering Star

A star with dreams to roam and play,
Bids the universe, "Let's be gay!"
It wobbles 'round, a tumble here,
Leaving trails of joy and cheer.

Meteorites chase with zealous glee,
"Catch us, we're faster than thee!"
The star just laughs, spins around,
While nebulae pulse, all unwound.

In this cosmic hide-and-seek,
Stardust whispers, "Come take a peek!"
Silly adventures with every turn,
Who knew the universe could burn?!

So if you spot a dancing flare,
It's just our star, without a care.
In ceaseless wander, it finds its place,
Spreading laughter through endless space!

Beneath Astral Canopies

Beneath the twinkling, winking lights,
Space critters hold their nightly rites.
A party in the Milky Way,
With laughter echoing in playful sway.

One comet brought a cake so bright,
Covered in sparkles, quite a sight!
While meteors served dance and song,
Aliens joined in, all along.

A black hole played peek-a-boo,
"Catch me if you can!" the black hole cooed.
While planets twirled in joy galore,
Smiling, happy, never a bore.

So if you gaze with wonder's eye,
Remember fun shines in the sky.
Underneath this astral dome,
Laughter and magic call us home!

Dance of the Celestial Traveler

In the sky a traveler pranced,
With sparkles on his shoes,
He danced through the Milky Way,
Leaving behind a trail of blues.

He bumped into a star so bright,
Who giggled 'Ouch, not so fast!'
They twirled around in cosmic light,
Their rhythm was a blast.

Asteroids joined in the fun,
Rolling with a rock-and-roll beat,
Planets clapped their hands, just one,
While meteors tapped their feet.

And when the jig was all done,
They bowed with a stellar cheer,
In the vastness, under the sun,
Who knew space could be so near?

Beyond the Tail of Time

A tail so long it wiggled and swayed,
Across the cosmos it jumped and played,
Time tried to chase with an angry pout,
But the tail just laughed, 'You can't catch me out!'

It looped through ages, a dizzying spin,
With giggles that echoed, 'Let the fun begin!'
Clocks got confused, lost in the race,
While the tail of time painted joy on each face.

A wormhole opened, a party inside,
With cookies and punch for the cosmic ride,
Time took a sip, then spilled it in glee,
Saying, 'Oops! Now I'm as messy as can be!'

So here's to the tail that wags with delight,
In the fabric of space, twinkling so bright,
Making each moment a splash of surprise,
Beyond the tail, oh how the laughter flies!

Cosmic Emissary

An emissary soared past the Moon,
On a mission to share a tune,
He whistled sweetly through space so wide,
Inviting the stars to join with pride.

Neptune chuckled, 'What's your song?'
Uranus chimed, 'We'll sing along!'
Got a chorus of comets in a bright parade,
Spinning round in a galactic escapade.

Mars brought snacks to fuel the cheer,
While Jupiter bragged, 'I can sing from here!'
The Milky Way shimmered with a cosmic glee,
As they all performed for each galaxy.

And when the night came to settle down,
The emissary bowed in a sparkly crown,
Said, 'Thanks for the jam, it was a delight!
You're the grooviest crew in this stellar night!'

Celestial Pathways

On pathways made of stardust and dreams,
Dancing alongside the solar beams,
Aliens giggled under the sun,
Racing each other just for fun.

One tripped on a meteor and tumbled down,
Rolling like a ball, he giggled and frowned,
But soon bounced back, with a cellophane grin,
Shouting, 'Space is crazy, but oh let's begin!'

They played hopscotch on Saturn's rings,
Creating games with celestial flings,
Black holes became swings, what a wild ride,
Laughter echoed across the cosmic tide.

As the day turned to night, stars began to play,
They put on a show, lighting up the way,
Each twinkle a wink, each blink a surprise,
In celestial pathways, fun never dies!

Echoes of the Night Sky

Up above, a big bright ball,
Shooting through like a playful call.
Whizzing past with a cheeky grin,
Sparks and laughter would begin.

Stars chuckle as it zooms by,
"Look at that, a milkshake sky!"
With sprinkles made of twinkling light,
It's a party, oh what a sight!

The moon plays tricks, the sun hides its face,
As comets run a silly race.
With tails that swirl and wiggle wide,
They dance around like kids outside.

So gather 'round, your eyes on high,
For cosmic jokes, they never die.
Each flash a wink from skies so grand,
A laugh that echoes across the land.

When Celestial Bodies Collide

Two planets met on a bumpy road,
Bumping heads, just like a toad.
With a plop and a splash, what a sight,
A cosmic pie fight in the night!

Stars burst out in giggles and glee,
As Mars threw a slice made of brie.
Jupiter joined with a banana flare,
Snack time in the astral air!

Comets giggled, taking a peek,
At the chaos that made them squeak.
With laughter loud, they bounced along,
In a universe that can't go wrong.

So when stars collide, grab your snack,
With cosmic munchies, you'll never lack.
Giggles and crumbs spread 'round the space,
In this wild celestial place!

Trails of Cosmic Dreams

There's a trail of sprinkles in the sky,
A sprinkle party, oh my oh my!
Dreams ride comets like a fun slide,
With giggles echoing side by side.

Asteroids dodge like they're in a game,
Chasing dreams without any shame.
With laughter ringing in the air,
Who knew space could be so rare?

Nebulae dressed in colorful threads,
Hosting banquets for sleepy heads.
With cupcakes made of stardust, too,
What a cosmic hullabaloo!

So wish upon a starry stream,
And ride the waves of your wild dream.
With a grin and a wink, let's make a toast,
To trails of laughter we love the most!

Luminous Tempest

A tempest brews, but not of rain,
Instead, it's chuckles worth the gain.
With lightning bugs doing the jig,
This storm is one that's rather big!

Galaxies whirl in a dazzling fight,
Spinning like twirlers in pure delight.
With thunder made of whoopee cushions,
It's a cosmic rumble that's full of notions!

Polar bears skate on solar rays,
In this tempest of giggles and plays.
With auroras dancing, bright and bold,
It's a tale of laughter, yet untold.

So buckle up for this funny ride,
As we laugh through the cosmic tide.
In luminous storms, we find our cheer,
With every giggle ringing clear!

www.ingramcontent.com/pod-product-compliance
Lightning Source LLC
Chambersburg PA
CBHW072142200426
43209CB00051B/258